Open Letters From Within

ALSO BY BIODUN ABUDU

Tales of My Skin

Stolen Sanity

Forbidden Scriptures

Open Letters From Within

Biodun Abudu

www.BiodunAbudu.com

Art Work Concept : Biodun Abudu
Graphic Illustration : Henry Jimenez

ISBN-13: 978-1-7335910-4-1

Dedicated to all the brave souls telling their stories as they begin their personal healing journeys to find freedom, happiness and love.

Pain

Recovery & Love

Extras

Pain

I knew I was on an interesting journey the first moment I ever shed a tear. Bathing in abuse, I was a bird in a cage. Soaked in tears and drowning in fear.

Gravity Hurts

I knew I was on an interesting journey

The first moment I ever shed a tear in my life

Grabbing weapons and tools to protect myself

Unfortunately I dived in naked and naive

Under the umbrella of what I called love

Love that wrapped me in a blurry atmosphere

Love that beat me black and blue but fucked me so good

I was left helpless, left to write letters to the universe

Unfortunately, there was no one to rescue me

Abused by my lover and mocked daily by his side chicks

They all uttered out words that knocked off my crown

Reality had splashed on my face but my soul was gone already

After so many years of being called a fellow man for not being pregnant

I finally do get pregnant and still it is not enough

I vent to my partner who responds with silence

Then I'm left to make decisions on my own

I'm forced to take away our blessing

I now live with the regret of taking away my child

Memories of An Imperfect Angel

From birth I took my queue behind every other sinner

Settling for the devil I gladly accepted every slap to my face

The slightest touch from a rain drop made me cry

Staying indoors and peeking from behind the curtains

Every foot step made me tremble, I was living in fear

Kneeling for forgiveness but I was lifted with an uppercut

The floor was like canvas and my blood and tears were the paint

I took a bow and watched my sanity taken away by my lover

Heaven is a day away as I counted down to my own death

I have now accepted that my soul is no longer mine to keep

Love is Blind

You left me to be run over by a car

You pushed me down a very high mountain

You left me to drown in the Atlantic Ocean

You shot my brains and forcefully ripped my heart out

You kept me from progressing, consistently causing traffic

You led me into a trap so I can be killed

You left me with no legs that and all I can do now is drag myself on the floor

You chopped off my hands so I couldn't reach out for help

You took my only breath away from my body

You took my eyes from seeing the truth

You took my only hope in believing that there is
still a reason for living

You pierced through my gentle soul with a thick
spear

You shoved me against the wall from seeing the
path to success

You placed me in a deep ocean, for me to drown in
my own tears

You placed my life on hold for you to find your own
happiness

You were my passion for life but now a terror lead-
ing to my death

Love That Hurts

Love brutally fucked me and my tears were its cum

It nutted all over my feelings and it mocked my sanity

It pushed me in a pool of insecurities to drown

I lacked the knowledge of my self -worth

I couldn't let go of my shelter and financial support

So, I gave love multiple discounts whenever it came

My legs opened wide despite my battered face

Love beat me black and blue but it fucked me so good

It's a love that manifested its wickedness into my blood

Walking around looking like a billboard full of scars, abuse and pain

Making pain look good and slaying with a fake smile

We cooked with unique utensils of destruction

We ate from the expensive plates of deceit, lies, pain and sorrow

Breakfast was served with verbal abuses and I couldn't walk away

At the confessional booth I continue to pray for freedom and strength

Only because I feel death waiting and lurking around the corner

Prayer For The Wicked

My scars are my hidden chapters
As I walked on shattered glasses
As I swam daily in my tears
As I walked past my fears and my doubts

Sleeping with the enemy
He took away my sanity
He took away my soul
He took away my joy and peace

I wish sorrow upon his life
I hope he would lay in worry
I hope he will have continuous discomfort
For he will feel the pain I felt, Amen

The 100 Partners Story

If we were allowed 100 partners
Would you take the offer?
To be able to pick anyone of your choice
Would you take the offer?
To be able to have sex with any of them
Again, would you take the offer?
Some of us would have been way past 100
Infact some of us would be on credit by now
There's a deep story behind the actual truth
Ladies deposits a part of their soul in you after sex
Men also leave a part of their soul in you after sex
It's beyond what our naked eyes can see
Intercourse unites two people's energies and spirits
Different energies or spiritual forces pollute the internal temple
Even condoms can't protect you from evil forces behind the flesh

Here is a warning from the other side
A story from the clouds above us
So, if we were allowed 100 hot partners
Really, we should be rejecting the offer

Tales of The Blood Moon

Two days ago, we were talking about our dreams and our plans

We toasted to a good life as we waited for the solar eclipse

As we stood on the rooftop there became an awkward silence

I suddenly asked about her family and it began a war zone

She is a good girl to many but a monster behind closed doors to me

She told me to kneel and pray to the lord above if I was tired of her abuse

I loved her even though she puts capital letters in my history of abuse

Kneeling before me and opening her robe, she forces me inside of her

She ripped my bible pages and used it as tissue to wipe my tears and blood

Still I stood by my woman despite my cries, pain and sad confessions

A War in Our Mansion

At the feet of my partner I surrendered to be a slave
Left in the dark, afraid to enter our doorstep
The medications given to me were to silence me
Helping anyone and everyone around us
But neglecting what was beneath our waters
Working 9 to 5 just to keep my partner entertained
While she fed me a balanced diet of madness
Securing the bag for her but not securing my sanity
I can't kill myself trying to make it right all the time
Even God himself rested on the 7th day

Letters from The Battlefield

Culture has taken the throne of God

Emphasizing that children are not brides

Crying when an elder lifts a cutlass at us

Raped beyond the point of recognition

Taking away our sanity and personal space

Depression running through our blood streams

Writing an essay for help and getting only an
"okay" response

A kid in pain and fighting forcefully to be heard

A mother forced to share her home with another
woman

A father fearful of showing his raw emotions before
anyone

A daughter stripped naked in the open and fighting
for her pride

A son punished and his dry mouth is starving from hunger

The devil taps on shoulders and saying there is no value for life

In anger, we spit on the graves of the ones supposed to protect us

Gasping for air, shedding tears as culture and tradition has silenced us

Looking up to the heavens and praying for a mighty miracle

Fuck Love

In our world of a perfect dream
We take steps slowly to enjoy every moment
I swore to myself that I would not leave
I'd rather go blind than see you with another

You swear to me that you will never leave
Like cutting each other and joining our blood in matrimony
I was on top of the world, soaked in love
Every kiss, every touch I never doubted

Was I wrong to love you and only you?
Just for you to cut me wide open
Your love and presence really made me blind
Blind to any doubts of you ever leaving

My Lips are Sealed

My lips are sealed and padlocked
Blood dripping from my mouth
Abuse has made its home here
Suicide has been on my thoughts

Being touched by older men
Without my personal consent
Smacking me to the floor to hush
For how long will it continue?

My light turned on away from him
My light was turned off seeing him
He whispered, saying it won't hurt
I had to get used to it with tears

Night after night I wanted to run away
Month after month I mentally collapsed
Year after year I wish he just died
So much damage placed upon my soul

No More Jays for Me

It's all lies the moment a man says his name is Jay
It's usually a rollercoaster of lies, deceit and games played
He has many boyfriends and girlfriends he cares for
He is always horny which is what is majorly known for

You send him a text and his response is "HI"
His "hi" response is better than when he says "who is this"
No matter what he remains the truthful one
I'm always the difficult one while he is the easy one

Words can not explain the pain and headache I get
He rather donate his time online than to me
He is always busy and foolishly I still stay
Anyone looking for pain and betrayal can go for a Jay

A Raging Libido

Sex to me is sort of a ‘calm down’ pain killer pill
Sex did help me at times pay all the damn bills
It was done uncountable times at my own will
If I didn’t have it right now, I could maybe kill

Sex satisfied me when I was very much hungry
Sex satisfied me when I was always very horny
Sex satisfied we when I was bored and lonely
Sex satisfied me when I was stressed and angry

Sex was like that force field that took my energy
Sex brought out the sultry, sexy and mad chemistry
Sex took its first place in my childhood vocabulary
Sex took away my honesty, pureness and virginity

Sex left me rather confused between love and lust
Sex gave me extra- curricular activities before I rust
Sex provided me a plate full of 13- inch dicks to
bust
Sex was my all in all, I needed to have it, it was a
must

Woman to Woman

You fucked me raw and nutted on my feelings
You were so cold to me, you had no feelings
I blame you for everything and I'm so suicidal
If only I listened to my friend's advice that was so vital

She said so many times close your legs to married men
I replied with so much anger, just saying “fuck you”
I repeatedly said “I’m not the one, never have been, never will be”
Always sitting on ready to fight but didn't take her advice

Woman to woman, don’t let destruction make a home in your temple
Woman to woman, take pride in who you allow access into your temple

I Celebrate You

I value your lies
I value you cheating on me
I value driving me crazy
I value your physical abuse
I value your verbal abuse
I value you not appreciating me
I value you taking away my self- worth
I value you raping me when I refused
I valued you sucking my energy dry
I value you making me insecure
I value you making me live in fear
I value you not loving me when I truly loved you
I value you always embarrassed of being seen with me
I value you telling me every morning that I am hideous
I value you telling me that I am a major failure
I value you telling me to die because I am worthless

All About You

You had me on lock down

Even when I found another path

I was truthful to you no matter what

Even when you fucked my best friend

The whole world asked me why

I answer because I am lost without you

Secretly I hope that one day you will change

I wondered why you treat me this way

I wait up till you get in at night, even when you tap me, I roll over

Sex in the morning, afternoon and night

I even agree when you say you want a threesome

I can't make you angry or I'll be living without you

You slowly throw me off my track

All because I want to be with you

You bring me to a suicidal point

A point where I'm just living with no purpose but just to please you

Wow, you got me good

I pray one day I'll find that very strength to at last leave you

I Plead

I willingly took a step further in our relationship
I took a chance to see what good will come out
I let you in my dimensional section of a soft layer
You clearly saw that I was extremely fragile

To satisfy yourself you ripped me open
You tore me open, giving me an unbearable pain
Physical resisting you I start pushing you back
Trying to tell you I want to stay protected

Your 20 second pleasure seems more important
Such an overpowering weight you forced on me
I plead for air as you compress your arms on me
I am hoping at this point you just get it over with

For the sake of the women in your life and let me go
I can feel an unpleasant pain with tears rolling down
I thought you were a gentle caretaker in the begin-
ning

Now all I see in my blurry view is a parasite eating me up

Surviving on my weakness for his pleasure with a smile on his face
I will tell my story of how you forcefully went in me to fulfill your satisfaction

Take Me Back

Take me back to a respectful era
Where our men opened the door for women
Lets go back to a time when privacy was a thing
Where our women kept their relationships private
Bring back the shows like Moesha
So we can watch something we can relate to
Take me back to the mother land
Where our neighbors became family
I would like to take a walk on memory lane
Through the love letters and family albums
Can I take a break from emails & text messages
So I can appreciate written letters once again

Writings on The Wall

I wonder why you don't try to treat me right
At least act like love me is that alright ?
You send me off on delivery like a USPS mail
You put my love in a prison cell, I need bail

It's a constant battle trying to win your love
We act like we're one but where is the love?
Loving you is a crime now as you stay busy
Treating me like shit while you stay busy

How did I fall in love with the devil, I wonder?
I need to find a way out, to move on
It's all about you as it has always been your com-
mands
I need a real love, searching for a love, "I'm in de-
mand"

It's now official I am a victim of daily abuse
I need to let it go and let go of my pain
It's way much better to be alone
Than to be dragged or drained with you

Uncountable Wishes

Today I turned a year older
I wish I could be given uncountable wishes
I wish I could back to being 11
To live without bills, truly to just be chilling
To climb over the fence to go to house parties once more
To have really spent more time with my grandparents
To write more and have kept my childhood photos and diary
Really appreciate those nightly walks
As adults sadly we barely even look up to the skies to see the stars
Can I go back and lose my virginity to someone more deserving?
Maybe attend that tv audition that I missed when I was 13
Can my wish take me even further back into the past?
Where I could convince the devil to apologize to God
So, we could go back to the Garden of Eden
I really miss being a kid who had the time to watch the lady bugs fly

To enjoy one more time watching my peers tie a thread on a dragon fly
To be a kid who threw stones to knock off a ripe fruit from a tree to eat
To redirect the younger me away from walking straight into trouble
To have saved money and to have invested
To have asked for stocks as a birthday gift instead of video games

Can I have the opportunity to tell the younger me to be more confident
On a deeper level can I ask my father why he left
Why he left me with my toxic single mother
Can I really mentally and truthfully forgive those that hurt me

The World We Live In

So much damage done in the name of God
Procreation is the first commandment in the Torah
Laying there like a log of wood waiting for you climb on top
We have to make a family whether it appeals to me or not

Power seems to take away sanity by making children brides
Forced into an arranged marriage then it turns to a polygamous marriage
Called the Whore of Babylon for wearing a mini skirt by church members
Told I'm going to hell for divorcing my abusive husband by my neighbors

If a man is raped, he should be happy it was free sex thrown at him
If a woman was raped, it was her fault
She was the one that tempted the man

Frenemies

Begging and bashing with the same mouth
Is like jealously that started north and ended south

To tarnish one's image in front others takes evil power and a cruel might
However, everything done in the dark surely comes to light

Don't say you have forgiven someone and truly moved on
When really you are secretly holding onto a grudge all along

People that shuffle friends around for their current beneficial needs
Are usually the people who are cursed and are forever going to be in need

A friend that can invite you on a group trip just to complete an Airbnb
Is a friend that definitely with no hesitation kill you in your deep sleep

Lastly and importantly a friend who is only loyal to their need of you

Is a wicked and selfish friend you should keep far away from you

Rape

Rape
Unlawful, Unwanted
Damaging, Frightening, Traumatic
Feeling broken with a dark cloud of memories
Abuse

R - Reoccurring trauma
A - Abuse
P - Painful
E - Eliminating ones sanity

Suicidal

Suicidal
Unhappy, Depressed
Considering, Withdrawing, Ending
A sad way to tell the world “I Quit”
Self - Destruction

S - Sad & self destruct
U - Unwanted & unhappy
I - Internal battles
C - Cry for help
I - Isolated thoughts
D - Depressed
A - Alternate escape & a way out
L - Lost & lonely

No 800,012

I was mad at God for letting the devil's servant damage me
I was mad at my parents for not being sympathetic and comforting
I was judged for my sexuality instead of comforted as a rape victim
It felt great to him but to me it set me onto a suicidal path
He had brutally broken into my temple
My temple which was guarded with a NO
My eyes filled with tears that came from within my soul
My mouth filled with blood and gushing out to the marble floor
My nose still remembers the heavy scent of the cigarettes
I still hear the echoes of the horrible words he used in my ears
I wouldn't even wish this on my enemy, not even for a minute
I may shove the memories or incident into a box to put away
However, the files are always revisited at some point of my life

It's like a permanent tattoo on my skin saying raped, raped victim or once raped
On my forehead when I look in the mirror, I see rape victim number 800,012
Maybe I'm destined to have depression place it's dark blanket upon my life
Trying my best to survive but I had family neglect glowing all over my skin

Boys' Quarters

Boys' quarters were the spaces in which helpers or maids were allocated to live

Today boys' quarters are where the master serves his penis to the house- maid

At times, it's where the madam of the house finds comfort with the male help

The male house help has no choice but to hush and serve his madam as asked

Drivers who need temporary accommodation stay in these quarters as well

The master's daughter suddenly finds accommodation in the driver's arms

Secrets are often hidden in these parts of the house or compound

Taboos are done in these quarters with a threat or sometimes with a bribe

Sadly, sometimes it is where the fearful house maid loses her virginity to the master

Unfortunately, she may be having the master's first child before his barren wife

Pussy on strike

When my man can't act right I put this pussy on strike

When his love turns wicked, I put this pussy on strike

If he is acting like he has lost his damn mind, I put this pussy on strike

If he doesn't appreciate me then I put this pussy on strike

If he disrespects me in public, Trust that in private I put this pussy on strike

If he is taking forever to claim you put your pussy on strike

If a man doesn't see your worth put your pussy on strike

Grab the wheels from him and put your dam pussy on strike

If he is always busy and doesn't take you as priority
put your pussy on strike

Take a break or a vacation, put him on probation
and put your pussy on strike

Blurry Visions

When it comes to love we ignore the clear signs
Even when person is married
Even when the person is a murderer
Even when the person doesn't speak our language, we still rely on body language
Someone filled with dark secrets, we still will want to give it a chance
Inside our private thoughts we can't resist such a wicked person
Our private parts have never been so wet
Our private parts have never craved somebody so badly
Though we know the person would break our hearts
The touch from this fellow we can't resist
Our emotions are far gone, gone to deep
When we know it's a mess but we still pray for it
We still are hoping for a change
Kissing another person, we still stay
Fucking their office assistant, we still stay
Even when he hugs and loves another man, we still stay
Long as we live, we will always love this fellow that broke our hearts
Everybody always has a say in our bedroom
Everybody has a say in our relationship

Placing call upon calls, text after text we get no response
Love suddenly hurts when we can't be with the one who got away
Love suddenly hurts when we can't truly be with the one, we truly love
In the very end, I still love this fellow because he is all the love I know

Dick on Lock

When I give to her and she don’t know to act I’ll put my dick on lock

When she can’t appreciate the glow I give her then I’ll put my dick on lock

If she is showing her friends my dick pic then I’ll put my dick on lock

If she is inviting her friends into our bedroom then I’ll put my dick on lock

If she is not ready to settle down then I’ll put my damn dick away and on lock

If she is acting like she ain’t a married woman then I’ll put my damn dick on lock

Open Letters From Within

Lady License

You can not browse without access
You can not ask to see my particulars
Especially if you aren't official
Set your standards lower if you have no substance
I’m a whole lot of woman
So, don’t aim too high for what you can't handle
No cake for a lazy man
You have to work, work, work to get this
Even when you get this you have to work to keep it
Don't touch what you haven’t earned
Action speak louder than words
When I see a real man in front of me
Just then you can have my lady license

Mother Africa

Dear Mother Africa, help your children that have turned cold
They have turned cold toward their brothers and sisters
They slay their own blood for the title that isn't theirs
They fight battles that are not even their own to begin with

They take every invitation to every unnecessary argument
Calling each other names that you have not given us from birth
Taking the lord's seat and judging others from their couch
Walking through wickedness and ending in self destruction

Keep them in your daily prayers as they are going astray
Save their souls, touch their heart before it starts to decay

Lekki Diaries

I'm always on route leaving Lekki to meet you in Yaba
And I never stopped to wonder if I have lost my mind
But you have always sacrificed your pocket money
And always had your chops dropped over to me

I guess this is how I measured your love for me
I gave you extra points for your good morning BBM pings
And you grab the extra credits with your good night messages
Because I'm inexperienced I weirdly list down the times we have had sex

We have had sex over 10 times now, so I think to myself I must be the one
I wait for you to look at me during lunch time and it gives me assurance
Smiling ear to ear and believing his brown eyes has told me so
When the slum book reaches me and you didn't mention me

I controlled myself and said to myself this is a private love, baby girl
However on our graduation it was clear, I was just a hole to feed your urges
So, when you said good bye I lost my damn mind and you killed my pride
In return I said bye and said “your father was better in bed” killing your pride

Amen

I fucking told you that I'm a sand castle but you stepped on me
Despite my daily devotion to love you, you still sent me packing
It's like I say I love you but in return your response is just an "ok"
Easy for you to demote me to friends after I gave you my temple

I dropped all to be with you ready to fight for you not matter what
Little did I know in return you didn't include me in your picture at all
I thought us being Nigerians you would be different but you're heartless
Like a sweet dream you told me I was the one for you every single day

Like a beautiful nightmare you slapped me out of my sweet sleep
You were the only topic in my life but you had many others in yours
Fuck your friendship you shove to my face, I can't stand your cruelty

It's like I have been raped just like you once were
but mine feels constant

You keep telling me no one cares for you in your
family now it's clear
It's clear that you are one that should have never
been born to hurt me
I hope the next person you hurt shows you how it
feels like to be me
One thing though what you did to me many will do
for you amen! amen!

Respect

Respect where you came from!
I don't mean your father's land
I mean the vagina you came out from
How dare you look me in the face!
How dare you point your fingers at me!
How dare you call me a bitch!
I was your entrance into this world
I brought you in and I can take you out
Respect where you came from

Alone with the Mirror

Baby bibs, toys and pacifiers are what the innocent kids yearn for
Little do they know they were born sinners according to the bible
No one can really explain to them the bills, heart break that's coming
No one can really tell them if they will be protected by their parents

Some married off at age 12, pregnant by age 13 and silenced for life
Some are told they are ugly, they are not worthy to be on this earth
That why what we all see in the mirror are completely different
I don't mean the obvious, I mean our personal self-worth views are different

What's been installed into our minds from a young age really has weight
It's from our alone times in front of the mirror that we begin to make decisions
Sometimes we even push ourselves to plastic surgeries or even suicide
The scar we see on our forehead in the mirror reminds us of the hurtful things

The mirror that's locked up in our bathrooms, bedrooms and purses is powerful
It serves as a reminder of where we are coming from and where we hope to go
It sometimes reminds us of the moment we weren't protected as kids
It unfortunately works a physical clock as our wrinkles stare back at us

Unspoken Thoughts to My Ex

Several years have gone past
Yet I still pray for him to change or to come back to me
I see he lives with his new partner
In the house we both picked out while we were together
I feel torn inside and I still hurt inside
Thinking of how his new partner enjoys every inch of that pipe
Thinking of how many times they both will say " I love you to" each other
The thought of him eating his partner out at the midnight hour upsets me
So, during these times I silently pray his partner dies
I love him too much to wish him death
But I hate him just enough to want him in a wheelchair
So I can come back into his life and keep him close to me

Lockdown

Welcome to an episode of being trapped
See the title "lockdown "is not related to a pandemic
It's being locked down in depression
Being dipped deep in abuse
A hell pit where my wife uses our kids to lock me down
If I try to leave I will never see them again
If I seek therapy she tells me I'm weak
She is in control of everything
This a woman who puts a gun under her pillow
I can't even get up to pee without being questioned
In all this when I ask of she loves me enough to change
She says I am to be answered and not to be questioned

Alone

The fear of growing old alone is very deep
Especially for those of us who are single
During the day we appreciate the perfect city views
However, at night we cry ourselves to sleep
Sleeping alone, tossing and turning with lots on our minds
Reaching a certain age with no love or no kids
At times, we are the constant third wheels amongst couples
The fear of growing old alone again is very deep
During a pandemic we are in a lockdown alone
If we get sick there's no one to cook for us
There is a certain fear to not be forgotten
There is a prayer to not slip and fall and be discovered months later

McShady

We all have that one shady mofo that acts up when the drive is so smooth, from paradise it turns to a battlefield or a mystery case. I ain't a crime solver or detector but I'm currently a bitch that has to address this glitch. So listen!

After numerous condoms years and after shower centuries it's still depressing that at your historical age you still can't understand the meaning of communication except when you are under my sheets. Quite pathetic, but I guess life doesn't guarantee smart or mature people all the time. Nigga you preached about maturity and being real but you presented the total opposite.

You baked a cake called "shadiness" and instead of going into world war 6 with you imma just give you a slice of the cake you baked. Now you don't exist on this earth as far as I'm concerned and if anyone asks me of your pathetic behind more than likely I will say "is that fool still alive?" .

It's so frustrating to walk a mile with a so- called adult and along the way I have to pat your doggy ears to know how you feel. It's extremely weird when you suddenly stop answering my calls, text messages. I mean after numerous kisses, movie tickets, dinner dates I'm still in a state of shock. I feel robbed of my precious time!

I will say I ain't a satisfaction post where you stick your tongue in when you want. I ain't a midnight snack that you munch on after late hours. The season has changed and your shady acts are not trending in my atmosphere anymore!

However I foresaw the future the very moment my lips touched your lips I kinda felt this electric flow and I knew you were gonna be trouble !. I still wanted to swim in this death pool of yours which was a pure waste of time, so I totally blame myself but it was cute for the 15 minutes, it lasted . . .

Save Our Souls

Dear God,

The world has gone crazy and those older than us have left the youth to venture into the cold world alone. The world says the youth are the future generation to take over. Indeed, we are, however when we seek for help there is rejection. We seek for therapy and support but instead some tell us to bend over.

We seek direction to success from elders but some lead us to death. We admire those older than us but instead of reaching out to help us some of them immediately see us as threats and suddenly become blind to our existence.

The world is so self- absorbed that youth cant share their stories. Living for today is what most are doing since no one cares to stop it. A lot of us youth roam the streets at 3am and it's not what you think, it's simply because we refuse to believe hell is a place called home. Tomorrow? Is not a word that exist since the truth has been hidden.

Trying to understand the state of mind of young one is impossible. Some of us wish we could just have someone listen to us but that's hard to find. When we do find someone to listen its usually after we have been stripped naked and have exercised our mouth to the pleasure of some elders. Those are usually the ones who after taking advantage of us, they boldly say the youth are "young, dumb and full of cum". A lot of us youth are risk takers, in fact we are entrepreneurs in the making. We go through life figuring out how to live our dreams since some of our parents or some elders think our dreams are foolish or will never be possible.

God can you please tell the world, some parents, some elders to never doubt what a young individual can become. Open my eyes, oh lord, to see a day when adults would be supportive of the young generation and put them on microphones to speak their mind, after all we will be the ones running the world till the next generation is ready.

If some adults were aware of our presence, I'm sure we wouldn't be having numerous teens that are pregnant. If they had us on their mind to sit down and advise us maybe a youth at age 21 wouldn't have slept with 32 people already at that young age. God please save the youth who is crying and feeling suicidal, touch his heart and bring happiness to his soul..............

Biodun Abudu

Recovery & Love

Don’t let anyone tell your story. Always remember healing is a personal journey. You have to find out what works best for you to heal, so you can move on into a new light. Once you have healed you can now settle and be at peace to enjoy your new found love.

To really love we must forgive ourselves for putting up with people that didn't appreciate our worth. We must find ourselves, love ourselves before loving someone. Even when you find love you should understand what needs to be done to keep it.

I Write

When I'm at war with myself I just write
True freedom for me comes through writing
Allowing me to remove thoughts of suicide and heartbreak
Releasing the pain that hides behind a smile

It's a moment where I take a deep breath
Opening my eyes with tears of joy rolling down
Assuring me, it's the beginning stage to overcome the pain.
I'm no longer giving my last speech on a cliff about to jump

Taking slow steps into the deep ocean of tradition
Becoming the voice for those who have been silenced by fear
I'm no longer being strangled behind closed doors.
Saying goodbye to pain, dark secrets, abominations and insecurities

Welcoming erotic day dreams, fantasies and love.
Bathing in my own flaws, my unknown and known sins

Speaking to My Father Above

Lord please tell me why does my heart hurt so much?
Why does it bother my soul when my heart is broken?
Why can't I forgive my mother for what she did to me?
Every time I see her phone number I get so upset
I wake up resenting my siblings for not getting involved
At night I bury curses specially made for my father on earth
Losing appetite is just one of the many things that happens
I literally lost hope in the beautiful possibilities
Because of this I was hesitant to love again
However, despite this, I am glad I found strength again
With you my father all things are possible
You gave me a reason to realize that my future has hope
Now I'm able to give myself a chance at happiness
Starting with the new love I have found in you
If I can't love myself how can I love someone else?
So I will be making a priority to love myself as well

Biodun Abudu

Where is the Love?

I learnt so much from my endless hook ups
Stroke a man's dick you can get him for a night
Stroke a man's ego you can get him for life
I applied this to my daily encounter with men
I felt safe and in control but it wasn't the best advice
Sometimes it just brought excess baggage from them
In today's world money can buy someone's time
Sometimes money can buy someone's love
I'm not willing to sell my love, time or my soul
I'm searching for someone worth my time and love
Someone who understand and appreciates the value of love
Someone who stimulates me mentally and spiritually

Child of Adam & Eve

Child of Adam and Eve
Return to the garden of Eden
Rise on your feet and look above your kingdom
Walk through the desert and through the evil forest
Swim through the rivers that uncovers the hidden truth
That's where the waters that washed the backs of our ancestors exist
Take along your queen and your children
Keep your head up high
Allow your queen to also lead and advice you
As knowledge knows no sex
Listen to the future that looks up at you
As wisdom knows no age
As you continue to make your way back
Do not look behind you
Child of Adam and Eve
Return to the garden of Eden

Biodun Abudu

Through the Storm

In a world where the truth has been hidden and diluted
One must be curious what's behind the hidden agenda
Our stories are locked away so that we remain unknowledgeable
our feet walk on floors where our ancestors once hit the ground from torture
Our souls connect together on the very spot where they knelt down and Prayed
They prayed for a better tomorrow which still seems far away
However, we continue to pray for our sanity to remain ours
Even though freedom is a word that is still foreign to our lips
We will continue to raise our kings and queens to rise above and succeed

Biodun Abudu

A Defined Queen

Someone once told me what a queen meant to them
She said a queen meant to be selective
Not every event was her cup of tea
It meant not being accessible to everyone
Working behind the scenes without expecting credit
Being someone, everyone wanted to know and work with
Becoming an individual that soaked themselves up with other cultures
Keeping down her body counts not discussing her bedroom affairs
A queen accepted all her flaws and appreciated her skin
Did not let her past define who they were
Kept it classy wherever she was
Her walk was subtle and graceful
She smiled to give millions hope
Through it all she was strong
In times of oppression she prayed to her maker
For he was the source of her strength

Family Values

Bring back the important moments within a family
Like setting up dinner tables for a family dinner
Weekend barbecues with distant cousins
Reintroduce me to grandma's cooking
Take away my comfort in fast food chemicals
Toughen me up with the fun shade aunty throws my way
Let there be a reason why I look forward to being home
Let home be a place I vent without judgment
Let me be able to have emotional intelligence
Let safe sex be a topic that is put on the table
After all my parents should be telling me right from wrong
Let me see the value in a family setting once again
Let's create a place where parents normalize apologizing to their kids
It's really hard to stay connected amongst the daily tasks in our personal life
But I promise to fight and continue to rebuild what was lost
If not for me I will do it for the sake of my children

Biodun Abudu

Human's Journey

Searching for love and laughter in my own journey
I've learnt to trust a soul of a man rather than his looks
Every opportunity is a lesson learnt even if its pain
For it is naturally human to make mistakes though
I have learnt to believe in every day as a new start
In hopes that trusting will lead to miracles happening
As well as believing my very dreams will come true
Though dreams could be fairytales and could be a lie
Today is one day of a person's life to make an attempt
Tomorrow is one day less to prove a point to someone
A week later could begin a new life chapter of a journey
A year past can in fact start something and be deep in it
In this human's journey I hope to share the air with love
I hope to gather the right tools to seek wisdom and truth
I will gladly like to end my homeless traveling and settle

In my journey I hope to locate a treasure that will be mine

Untitled

Like a fountain of water it flows endlessly
Like the skies it's here to stay everyday
Like death its unpredictable it comes unexpectedly
Like a shooting star or meteoroid, it can move really fast
Like a house it brings two or more people together
Like the sun rays it touches everyone
It's a natural gift which is given to humans and animals
It brings a smile upon a fellow's face
It makes a person at times speechless
It's the heart that it has a home and a place in
It seems like a spell when you do things you have never done before
It's very warm but when mishandled it has a cold side
It's very light but when broken it weighs in pounds
It's not when you go online searching for the hottest tom, dick and harry for sex
It's something that is celebrated and it occurs in special memories
When broken at times it shatters and it leaves you saying "I am through with it"
If you give it a chance and let it lead the way it will lead you to the right person

Just then you can sing those special songs while enjoying social moments
However I still wonder will it come way or least come true for me ?

He is……

He keeps me warm with his love
He keeps me uplifted with his trust
He keeps me happy with his blessings
He keeps me going with his protection
He keeps me assured with mighty wisdom
He is the reason my enemies can't figure me out
He is the reason I am alive and healthy each day
He is the reason many ask "how do you do it?"
He is the reason that curses return back to sender
He is the reason for all my success and completed goals
He will be the reason I will become a trend setter in my field
He will be the reason I will have many more years to come
He is the reason I will never know the words "I can't do it"
He is the reason I remain simply talented
He is the only creator of the world
He is the only "I am that I am"

Biodun Abudu

I'm Reborn

I have learned to walk by faith
I continue to put my pen to paper
I have gone the wrong route
I neglect daily negativity and wish my enemies well
I may have been that used product of yesterday
I'm reborn so I declare myself a virgin of today
Being reborn is to wake up anew of yesterday
It's a new awakening of my day not doomsday
One day is all it took for me to say no to failure
Failure is totally like a random one- night stand
That's why I stand clear of such
In fact, run away full speed from it

Biodun Abudu

Rated Safe

It is the main duty of the mother to protect her child
Pedophiles conquer hopefully it won't be with your child
A child turned teenager should know what's definitely wild
However, it's left for you to bring it from wild to sane mild
A lady emotionally abused shouldn't go hay- wire and loose
Keep your dignity and have some class don't be a free cruise
Know if he truly loves you and is in love with you, only you
However, keep an ongoing communication between you two
The spread of diseases comes from greed to have endless sex
To stay safe, you either find one lover or simply abstain from sex
Finding a committed lover is like finding a needle in the sand
Knowing this you must be willing to keep tight like a rubber band

Its ok to be freaky with one but not sneaky with the country
Sex is a human activity and better with one you call your own
Hook ups are a beginning process of becoming lost in the land
Rated safe is ending destruction from becoming countless like sand

A Future Plan

Elimination is the first step to become a career- driven person
Imagination sets you apart to becoming a creative person
Attention is the weapon for when you're a competitive person
Domination lets others watch and learn from the successful person

If you haven't mentally achieved your goals, it's not realistic
You have got to accomplish your goals to remain Fantastic
By not following the crowd and making history is Futuristic
Having one set path to success is what I call monopolistic

Distractions are only a part of life so you have to be focused
Successful stories of others will help you so remain inspired
Rejections are only humane but I know I'm hot and blessed

Haters do their full- time job giving me a reason to be touched

Don't be all talk no action put people to shame with a future plan
Success doesn't come easy so keep at it and do the best you can
If you're the type that gives up after a failure then you're not a man
Begin your career and end the job because time waits for no man

Relationship Thoughts

Respect should be from me to you to able to stayed connected
Trust between us will make either one of us feel less rejected
Communication is the key when we both talk to stay corrected
Consistency is essential like using condom to stay protected

Passion is a mystery that only us two can decode in our world
Love between us can flow endlessly and fly high in our world
Sex can be over rated between us two after all its own world
Kisses should be shared between us to dwell in our own world

Unity will make us go high, far away and move many mountains
Pure love for us is like an endless flow of water from a fountain
Time for us is laying together like it's like an intimate vacation

My heart will be a passage for you to have access to
my dominion

Commitment is being honest and faithful and free of
any deception
Careless individuals can come and go but you can
resist temptation
Our goal together hand in hand is trying to build up
a generation
So, I can stay steady in your future life to release
your daily tension

Online Lover

Is it you that I seek for a lifetime of love
and is it you that was sent from above
I am dying to know and meet you in person
I sense this connection like hands to glove
Behind the internet we wrongly interpret
I wait long for a reply and my heart begins to beat
You log off and it seems like my heart's been bro-
ken
Like I've lost my chance at finding true love
It might be strange and might be crazy
but you know you are also feeling me
A mystery of love waiting to be solved
So let's upgrade from me, you, to we and us two

Best Friend

I'm looking at him in awe of one of God's beautiful creations
He says I am so very tender with my words not to mention
I wish to take a journey into his mind and see a preview of his passion
That way I could find all the hidden truth of his emotions

I find happiness in him in fact my dreams are all about him
I day dream of him and every day is a deja vu of only him
I imagine us becoming one and in connection because I love him
Litle does he know my love is secretly dedicated to only him

I feel if there was anyone I would want to be alone with
I'm sure the answer would be very clear when I stay by him
it would be to obvious I guess as I blush dramatically

His name, his face, his everything is all I dream of
day to day

He told me once to guard my heart but still display
love
But how could I love someone who dims my light, I
replied
I wondered why he won't just fill in the spot I ask
of him
But the truth he finally reveals is that I'm just his
best friend

Countdown 2 Love

10. We see each other time to time. Now it's time to make a move as those other people are okay but we both together will make top class.

9. I'm well established and all I need is your name and for you to explain your status a little bit more

8. Like a job we test drive each other, a bit of fronting, looking good for one another. Dressed to impress and question each other I mean it's cool because cos it's all part of dating

7. Texting, calling, emailing using all communication links possible. We are used to staying in our own selfish domain during this cycle of getting to know one another.

6. Letting each other explore our words we suddenly let go of our put- up walls

5. Assuring each other that it might work. We go further sharing personal experiences. I believe you have gotten the job so you can begin working.

4. Taking you as my first priority and personal duty. I keep the tempo upbeat and head strong. Playing my role and making sure I am turning you on without being to commanding.

3. Giving you the wheel I let you drive, keeping me safe and secure without any doubts

2. Suddenly there is a promotion especially when you tell me how you really feel.

1. Finally ! At last! After all, and without a doubt. I was your current job but now I'm pronounced your one and only and till death do us part.

I Don't Deserve You

I been searching for love for the longest
I finally found it and I'm still the saddest
Only because I don't deserve such a love
I want to break it off but I'm truly in love

I suppose I just don't know what to do with it
My lover keeps saying "you'll be fine I know it"
But I have truly lost the true use of my heart
I guess I don't believe love matches my heart

I doubt myself but I feel so alive when I see you
I wish I could have this moment for life, I like you
I said like just because I'm not in love yet at all
When I'm in love you will know and I will tell all

I will market our love for a generational tale
To show all how love can make a full tale
I'm just going to let it go and live the life of love
Set myself free, walk hand in hand with love

My Drug

Your Blue jeans, my white t-shirt
Your leather jacket, my lace underwear
Your scruffy beards, my scarlet red lipstick
My smooth skin, your vintage camera
Our dreams, our happiness
Your smile is my mission
My joy is your passion
Your love is my drug
And I'm ready to risk it all

Biodun Abudu

Prince Knight

I'm patiently waiting for my very own special prince knight
The very caring one that will surely change my wrongs to right
I'm very independent, I got my own cars but I need a passenger
Looking for someone to get old with and share life with happily

I want to be stuck to only one lover of mine like glue, I mean super glue
I want to care for you and give you my all and write love songs to you
I want to travel the world with my prince knight holding his hands all through
I want to be soaked in love that all I can see in the blue sky is his reflection

Biodun Abudu

That Kind of Love

It's a mystery when the world can't figure out the connection
When two people have a new kind of love with its own definition
Day to day they dedicate their journeys into each other's dimensions
Obtaining a special key into each other's secret hidden dimensions
Both are joint creative forces and produce such great musical tools
People hate and talk but history says silence is the best answer for fools

Love Wins

Life and Unity
Outstanding Adventure
Very Protective
Endless Journey

Withstanding Tribulations
International language
Natural Affection
Special Bond

Love is life and unity
Love is an outstanding adventure
Love is very protective
Love is an endless journey
Love is withstanding tribulations
Love is an international language
Love is having a natural affection
Love is supreme and is a special bond

Biodun Abudu

Sacred Features

Skin color so dark and lovely it stands for one love
The nappy hair is a testimony to our original roots
Our hearts guide us and teach us to embrace our differences
Kissable curves and big hips that tells a story
Succulent and thick lips that speaks nothing but the truth
Natural breasts that are a testimony to visual appetites
A behind that jiggles and swings causing traffic along the way
The rewind button was created in honor of this natural behind
Soft skin that embraces the past and looks forward to the future
Eyes that has seen the human's journey and is hopeful
Ears that listen to our mothers as they pass on wisdom to us
A smile that whispers the international language of a love
Fingers that have protected and guided our future generation
Feet that walks away from our enemies but walks towards our father's kingdom

Biodun Abudu

Woman

Woman
Beautiful, Strong
Loving, Leading, Protecting
The Future is Female
She

Once Again

Based on our previous experiences
Some of us have ruled out all men
We think they are all dogs and cheaters
However, some men are testimonies
Sent from above like some will say
A well- mannered man truly does exist out there
One that will walk with you, side to side
A man who places you right beside him
A king that puts his queen by side and not behind him
A man that provides emotional nutrients to our soul
A man that gives love that covers us from head to toe
He lives in the present and will care for you despite your past
A man that trusts the that future is already sealed
His actions alone open the path to happiness
and through their presence you once again believe in love

You Will Always be Around

After several years of searching and praying for love
We unfortunately come to a conclusion about love
We suddenly think it doesn't exist and it's a fairytale
Some of us are negative to marriages calling it a fairytale

Then like a thief in the night it comes out of nowhere
In our darkness, a light shines on us out of nowhere
Suddenly confidence comes into your life again
It creates a moment where you can trust again

Love sets your spirit free just being in their presence
This is someone you thank God for their existence
When they make love to your soul it's like fireworks
Even without them proposing, your soul has said yes

That's why in sickness and in health you will always be around
Even for better or for worse you will still and always be around

Biodun Abudu

My Dear Friend

I have a friend who really is just a friend
He is not a friend with benefits, he's just a friend
We have never done anything sexual
Though we joke and playfully flirt a little
This certain friend of mine is different
He is someone I can share anything with
Because with family there can be judgments
With friends in my age circle there can be jealousy
This friend of mine has been there, done that
Giving me friendly advice that comes from his experiences
Who needs to go to a happy hour when the drinks can come to me?
When we drink, we share our life experiences, goals and dreams
The moments we share with wine glasses in our hands are priceless
Even though I may wake up on the kitchen floor, I appreciate it all
I appreciate being completely me around my dear friend
I can be awkward, I can be silly, in fact I could let one rip in front of him

Biodun Abudu

I Claimed and Received

I have always heard about love at first sight
I never did really believe it until it happened to me
It hit me like a love potion or some kind of spell
I was blushing, something that was foreign to me
I tripped over things that were not there on a flat surface
I couldn't walk properly, my knees were weak
When he asked me for my name, I forgot my own name
I just responded with a smile then he blushed and stared into my eyes
Suddenly everything around us didn't matter
In that quiet moment I said a prayer in my mind
I said lord "let this beautiful man be the one"
Then I stopped my myself and said "Thank You, God"
I took it upon myself to believe in the lord's gifts
So, I claimed and received this beautiful man
It was a beautiful love story
Every day since then has been worth celebrating

Biodun Abudu

'Till Death do us Part

Come here let me wash off the pain and abuse from your past
If the world robs you of your blessings
I'll be here to support you
When you come straight from the battlefield I'll be here waiting for you
Know that I will be by you side no matter what is thrown at you
Let me keep you warm despite the world's coldness
Let me empower you when society treats you unfair because of your skin color
When the journey is rough, I'll be here to say a prayer with you
Let me build a bridge to your heart and love you like your supposed to be loved
No matter what happens I'll always be here till death do us part

Biodun Abudu

From the Other Side

We are part of something way bigger
Our love has become stronger
We have a balance that keeps us together
I gain my power when you're around me
I get jealous at the way you love because I am yet to understand love
The way you love me, defend me is a mood 4 eva
Today I promise you that the scars on your body will be a thing of the past
There will no longer be a reason for you to feel you're in danger
The stars will always be there to guide you
So, if you are ever lost I am confident you will find your way back
You will always have the keys to the kingdom
My brown skin girl you already know what's mine is yours
There is no need to ask to drink from my water
I feel at home whenever I'm with you
I surrender my love to you
Ready to get married and say "I do" by the River Nile
I do fear something will happen to me soon
So, If something does happen to me

I know my spirit will always guide you and our child from the other side
You can always look up to the sky and see me smiling down at you

Rose Like..................

There is no manual for being in a relationship
However, your relationship should be private
During arguments accept your faults in the problem
Remember it's not a community- based project
Be aware that not everyone is happy for you
Do not tear down the image of your partner to the public
You know your partner the best in and out
So, get on your knees and pray for better days
Try to make it work so you're not part of the divorce statistics
Love is like a rose with thorns preserved in an amazing glass

Biodun Abudu

No Mountain High Enough

On earth there is none like you
You give me the moon and the sun
Even if I'm on mars you would travel from planet X to see me
Your love is stronger than any gift given to me by the Gods
Through valleys, seas and mountains you make it possible
If I were to find myself in the bottom of a whale's belly
I'm pretty sure the connection we have will lead you to me
When we make love the stars above change their colors in excitement
Even beings from other dimensions tune in with a telescope
You are exceptionally beautiful and perfectly crafted
I am thankful for your commitment in my life

Biodun Abudu

Mother's Love

The special bond between a mother and a child is sacred
Bonding is also necessary between the mother and her child
One that not so many people can't understand
which is probably why maternity leaves are so short
It still baffles me how men determine the length for maternity leaves
A mother's love is forever present and developed from the bonding
It doesn't affect her lost time away to be able to provide for her child
Because regardless of how far she goes the child will always know
The child will always remember the voice of his mother
He or she will always recognize the smell of his mother

Biodun Abudu

I Love You

I - Irreplaceable

L - Legit
O - Open hearted
V - Vow
E - Everlasting

Y - Yearning
O - Open
U - Understanding

Biodun Abudu

Life with You

Your true connection with me is the perfect way
You and the sunshine are what I need to start my day
Your physical presence just leaves me speechless
Your frame on my frame is the most artistic creation known today

Burning through my body like a volcano lava you give me fever
Coming down with intense heat like the African sun you give me fever
Sweat glides down my body and I begin to burn from your temperature
No matter how cold the world is, I have you to keep me warm

I can't go on without you in my daily life because you give me direction
With you I have assurance, because I know there is a guaranteed protection
Sparks fly when we are together, it's like love found a new real definition
If I was to live this life again, I will choose you again without hesitation

Biodun Abudu

Bio Fever

I never knew I possessed such a sensual luring bio power
It makes his warm heart pound and race even harder, faster
It's like I have the access to drive him crazy without caution
I need to be careful not to have him blow up in an explosion

I drive him nuts when my text comes in hrs and hrs much later
When I put it on him, it's like a new year's resolution to go harder
I take it to another level when I fulfill his fantasy and desire
I'm so destined and determined to make him pour like water

Red hot like the volcano cave, the atmosphere become steamy
After we feel well rested the moment is sky blue a bit dreamy
I might have skipped a process in our relationship process or life

But it's only natural that the fever takes us to another level in life

I'm about to take over his heart the best way I truly know how
Being real is the way to do such a job, to make him say wow
I alone can control the bio fever of the century in his world
The world we share to embrace love, fever and adventure

God's Response

Amongst millions of beautiful individuals out there
You sought me out to be yours only
This alone melts my heart
You are beautiful in and out
I appreciate you
I give thanks to God every day for you
Not only are you my lover but you are my best friend
You are such a rare soul
My number one supporter
Even when I doubt myself you uplift me
You take my hand and walk right beside me
This confidence you give me is amazing
Your presence in my life is God's response to my prayers
That why I will forever be thankful for you in my life

Biodun Abudu

The Sugar in My Tea

You are indeed all of the things that I hoped for
Someone that makes me feel good inside
Smiling from ear to ear
Glowing when leaving my house
At the mention of your name I start to blush
In the next life I will certainly choose you again
You are my sunshine and my moon light
Like my fellow Nigerians say "the sugar in my tea"
I'm indeed blessed
You celebrate me and I celebrate you
We build together, protect each other
We give a new definition of what it is to be loved
Your love is my peace on this earth
Through the chaos I find redemption in you
Your soul is pure and it opens the path to my happiness

Biodun Abudu

I do

You sing to my soul when you say “I love you”
Giving me assurance when you say it’s just “me and you”
When you have to go, I become sad and I just say “it’s cool”
A new found love they say but you have always been my sun and my moon
Gone are the days I ate alone, now it’s a table for two
I knew I couldn't live without you
Infact I rather die young than live my life without you
So that's why you got on one knee, without hesitation I said “I do”

Biodun Abudu

Ungodly Hour

At this ungodly hour
I vow to satisfy the love of my life
Leaving my innocence in the wedding hall
He already had paid my bride price
So I'll give him my body, mind and soul
There's nothing he carries that's too big for me
There's nothing I have that is too much for him
The fear of growing old alone is in the past
I've finally found someone special at last
And when he offends me I get so angry
But he apologizes when he is in between my cheeks
Loosing track of time, when we are together
Laying in bed together appreciating one another

Biodun Abudu

Extras

Straight Confusion

Your intentions are a mystery
Your past is unknown to me
What I see is brown sugar
And want it all to myself
However its bad and it's dangerous
A handsome interruption
The kind that is already in someone's cup
How do I get over our differences
The fact that your straight and I'm not
Your interest in me has me speechless
Your desire to be close to me
Makes me nervous
The signs are there
But I can't make the first move
If we do act on it
It will be our little secret
Or it could break some hearts
Either way I'm ready
I'm ready to pray with you till the end
I'm ready to risk it all
But only if you give me the go signal

Label Lover

I have finally found him and he is all mine
He has all the physical features he is so fine
I'm ok with all his tattoos that define only him
His initials I have tattooed to my heart boldly

He has never hurt me and has brought happiness
When I hold him tight, I exude so much richness
Other similar men try their best to lure me away
Even women try to tempt me at fashion runways

His chestnut skin color is so sexy in the sunlight
I love him in my arms as I board my plane flight
He is so popular and consistently in the news
I'm fabulous, he is classic we make a great news story

Fashion wouldn't be without him I totally swear
I plead for him to always be so very close and near
I can't take my eyes off him for a minute or an hour
I love him and I must confess his name is **LV**

Biodun Abudu

Story of My Heart

When he doesn't call me I panic
Not seeing his text has me distraught
What's crazy is that we are not even dating
Yet he has this hold on me that I can't explain
If I could spend the whole month with him
I would over and over again
How I wish I was on lock down with him
Then I would have found something special
A unique love in the midst of the covid pandemic
I can't even tell you when last I spoke to my mother
And here I am worried over a text from a friend
Only because she causes me pain
Her phone call steals my inner peace
Her words steal my sanity
When I'm left alone he is there for me
In a way that my long term friends are not
He supports me in a way that my family can't
I can't have him to myself even if I tried
Because I'm gay and he's just my straight friend

Biodun Abudu

Questions To The Man Above

Lord I have questions that I need to ask you
I really hope you understand
It's not meant to question your authority
I just want proper knowledge
I need insight as your child
Tell me my father
According to the holy bible
Since Adam and Eve were created first
And were the only ones around
Does it mean we are all brothers and sisters?
Because I can only think of the word "incest"
Lord you created everything
So you had to see the angel would turn to a devil
You had to see his betrayal in advance
You had to know eve would eat from that tree
I also want to know where were the dinosaurs?
Were they on Noah's ark ?
Did they die off before you created Adam & Eve?
What skin color were Adam and Eve ?
Are there other beings made in other planets ?
Please what is truly in the center of the earth ?
Tell me what happened to all the giants
If the devil apologized would you forgive him?
Would you reveal where the Garden of Eden is
What are the secrets of the all pyramids

What is hidden at the bottom of our waters
Lastly, what secrets are hidden in the Antartica

Honor Thy Parents

Honor thy father and mother they say
Yet my father is absent from my life
He didn't even look back
Not even a phone call on my birthday
My mother has become my enemy
Constantly attacking my pride
Stealing my sanity
I can't even stand to be in her presence
I didn't know Satan had been overthrown
Their vibe is toxic and draining
It sounds bad but I just can't
They were supposed to protect me
But they have abandoned me
They hold a knife to my neck
I can't honor my father and mother
If society could walk in my shoes
They will also run from pain
Pain that is pure hell
Hell that expects you to honor

Kele Kele Love

Lowering my standards
Because your handsome
You give me love in bits
I am kept as a secret
Only to be called after hours
Given the last piece of your attention
After your baby mothers
And after your online crushes
Loosing sleep over you
Shedding tears because of you
I love you but enough is enough
If I cant have you there's no use
If I have to hide to be with you
Then there's no point
Reaching out to you a day after
Yet I'm told it's a tad bit too soon
I can't just be your friend
With you expecting my legs to open
At your convenience
I am way better than this
My life can't be all about you
I am worth way more than this
I no longer want your kind of love

Biodun Abudu

Adam and Steve

This new era is quite interesting
We are questioned about our sexuality
Like it is necessary to know
But they use it to know how to place you
Society feels the need to be in our bedroom
Asking personal unnecessary questions
When you do confirm they seem surprised
That love between two men can be real
They expect you to say
"I gave him my heart and he gave me an std"
Little do they know I'm loving all of my man
I'm his man and he is my man
I'm his adam and he is my steve

Torn Internally

They say
Emotional infidelity
Is just as bad as physical infidelity
Once you give up your heart
Your going to give up your parts
I lost a good man
All because I wanted material things
I was distracted by other things
He offered me what many couldn’t
He loved me body and soul
Yet I betrayed him
I really lost a good one
Now my heart aches
And my soul cries
I really lost a good man

Biodun Abudu

The Bisexual Dillema

The worst thing a bisexual man can say
To his male partner
Is “well are you going to give me kids”
Then suddenly the relationship is over
After so many years
Loving a bisexual is not easy
You don't know who they are looking at
They watch women's asses and boobs
As well as men’s abs and chest
It’s mental draining to not know
Who he has interest in, as you walk together
Gay men hurt as much as women do
However, we can’t compete with pussy
And when we cry he expects us to man up
Oh! and that he doesn't do pity parties
Hanging up and moving on to someone else
Not sure if it’s a man or woman
But it hurts either way

Biodun Abudu

Dear Future Lover

To love me may not be easy
But know I will be here to stay
I'll be here to support you
And to celebrate all your wins
I won't ask for too much
Just make me laugh
Keep me smiling no matter what
Don't ever leave my side
I don't care about the material things
I just care about our privacy
I'm ready to travel the world with you
Ready to make so many memories
When I cry, it will be because I'm thankful
I will be blessed to have you by my side
Just know that I am an energizer bunny
Especially during the ungodly hours
Let me add that Im the type to meet you at the door
With nothing on, just skin
But seriously I can't wait to meet you
Grow old with you and die with you
P.S I love you

Some Men

Some men won't apologize to women
Especially their female friends
Unless their dick is involved
They won't go above and beyond
Until you open your legs up for them
It's really sad but sometimes it's the truth
No respect is given to women
Until they have had an opportunity
To conquer your body
They are insensitive towards your feelings
But are sensitive when their dick is in
And it's about to bust a nut
What I'm I even saying
Even if you give it up
It still doesn't guarantee anything
That's when some go ghost on you
They even leave you on read
They will even mock you for having feelings
They will not apologize for leading you on
It's cold out here in these streets
Ladies ! Know you worth
And protect your feelings
Because some of these men ain't shit !

Thank you so much for being open to reading this book. I hope you enjoyed reading it as much as I enjoyed writing it.

You can find me on Instagram @BiodunAbudu and also on Twitter @BiodunAbudu

Feel free to write me at info@biodunabudu.com

Acknowledgments

A special thanks to the following people:

Carol Tietsworth

Henry Jimenez

Kashiera Franklyn

To My Sister, Oyinda

You all made this poetry collection possible !

ABOUT THE AUTHOR

Biodun Abudu was born in Rhode Island, but comes from a Nigerian background. He wrote his first title "Tales of My Skin" based on a true life story in 2011. He then released his second title "Stolen Sanity" in 2019 which is also based on a true life story. His third book "Forbidden Scriptures" was released in 2020. When he is not writing, he works as an Artist. In 2011, he graduated with an A.S. degree in Fashion Design, and a B.A. in Merchandising Management with an emphasis on Fashion Merchandising. He currently resides in New York City.

Twitter : @BiodunAbudu
Instagram : @BiodunAbudu
Email : Info@biodunabudu.com
Website : www.BiodunAbudu.com

www.ingramcontent.com/pod-product-compliance
Lightning Source LLC
Chambersburg PA
CBHW032112090426
42743CB00007B/332
9781733591041